GALE
CENGAGE Learning

Novels for Students, Volume 43

Project Editor: Sara Constantakis Rights Acquisition and Management: Robyn Young Composition: Evi Abou-El-Seoud Manufacturing: Rhonda Dover

Imaging: John Watkins

Product Design: Pamela A. E. Galbreath, Jennifer Wahi Digital Content Production: Allie Semperger Product Manager: Meggin Condino © 2013 Gale, Cengage Learning

For product information and technology assistance, contact us at **Gale Customer Support, 1-800-877-4253.**

For permission to use material from this text or product, submit all requests online at **www.cengage.com/permissions**.

Further permissions questions can be e-mailed to **permissionrequest@cengage.com** While every effort has been made to ensure the reliability of the information presented in this publication, Gale, a part of Cengage Learning, does not guarantee the accuracy of the data contained herein. Gale accepts no payment for listing; and inclusion in the publication of any organization, agency, institution, publication, service, or individual does not imply endorsement of the editors or publisher. Errors brought to the attention of the publisher and verified to the satisfaction of the publisher will be corrected in future editions.

Gale
27500 Drake Rd.
Farmington Hills, MI, 48331-3535

ISBN-13: 978-1-4144-9486-9
ISBN-10: 1-4144-9486-6
ISSN 1094-3552

This title is also available as an e-book.

ISBN-13: 978-1-4144-9272-8
ISBN-10: 1-4144-9272-3
Contact your Gale, a part of Cengage Learning sales
representative for ordering information.

Printed in Mexico
1 2 3 4 5 6 7 17 16 15 14 13

The House of the Scorpion

Nancy Farmer 2002

Introduction

The House of the Scorpion (2002) is a novel by Nancy Farmer, a celebrated author of science fiction and fantasy for young adults. It is set about one hundred years in the future, when Mexico (renamed Aztlán in this future time) and the United States have each turned over part of their border territory to a group of drug lords, who produce drugs freely in the land they call "Opium" while they keep people from crossing the borders illegally. The novel interweaves a recognizable not-too-distant past, as the residents of Opium live without computers, cell phones, and other modern conveniences, and a frightening future, when cloning and interfering with people's brains to make them into compliant workers are taken for granted. The protagonist is Matt, a clone created from the tissue of El Patrón, the wealthiest and most powerful of the drug lords. As he ages to adolescence, Matt struggles to determine his identity and his worth, as a clone and as a human, and tries to find friendship and family.

The House of the Scorpion, Farmer's third Newbery Honor Book, also won the National Book Award. It has been translated into at least seven languages, including Chinese, French, and Slovenian.

Author Biography

Farmer was born on July 9, 1941, in Phoenix, Arizona, the youngest of three children of Frank and Sarah Coe. At the age of three, she caught measles from her sister Mary; to make amends, Mary taught Farmer to read at a level far beyond her years. However, dyslexia kept Farmer from doing well in school. By the time she was nine, her father was running a hotel in Yuma, Arizona, near the United States–Mexico border. Farmer helped out at the front desk and made friends with cowboys, railroad men, and other travelers. Many days, she skipped school to explore the desert and the banks of the Colorado River, but she read all of the books and magazines left behind at the hotel and eventually found her way to the public library.

After graduating from Reed College in 1963, Farmer took a two-year Peace Corps assignment in India. For a few years after returning, she worked in a biology lab at the University of California, Berkeley. In 1972, she went to Africa, where she lived for seventeen years. First she lived in Mozambique, where she worked as a chemist and entomologist. Next she went to Zimbabwe to work on tsetse fly eradication; in 1976, she met literature professor Harold Farmer in Harare, Zimbabwe, and they married. When she was forty years old, Farmer enjoyed reading books to the couple's four-year-old son, Daniel, and decided to try writing. The quality of her work was quickly recognized, and her second novel, *The Ear, the Eye, and the Arm* (1989), first published in Zimbabwe, became a success in the United States as well when it was reissued in 1994; it was named a Newbery Honor Book, among other recognitions. In 1988, Farmer and her family returned to California, where she wrote and sometimes took work as a lab technician. By 1992, she was able to write full-time.

As 2012 drew to a close, Farmer had published ten novels for young adults in addition to four picture books, and her work had been published in twenty-six languages. Three of her novels, *The Ear, the Eye and the Arm*; another novel set in Africa, *A Girl Named Disaster* (1996); and *The House of the Scorpion* (2002), were named Newbery Honor Books; *The House of the Scorpion* also won the 2002 National Book Award for Young People's Literature. Between 2004 and 2009, she published the three novels in the Sea of Trolls series before beginning to draft a long-promised sequel to *The House of the Scorpion*. She and her husband lived in Menlo, California, near the Cargill Salt-works, which she used as the model for the shrimp-harvesting factory in *The House of the Scorpion*.

Chapters 1–5: Youth: 0 to 6

The House of the Scorpion opens in a laboratory, where human embryos are being grown in petri dishes. Only one survives long enough to be gestated—in a cow's uterus—and "harvested." Ordinarily, the newborn would have its brain damaged intentionally to dull its intelligence, but because this one is "a Matteo Alacrán," it is spared. Five years later, that newborn is a boy named Matt, who lives with a woman named Celia in a small house surrounded by poppy fields. Celia is a cook in the Big House, and when she goes to work each day, she leaves Matt alone with the doors locked and the windows nailed shut. There is a clear bond of love between Matt and Celia, but she will not allow him to call her *Mamá*, explaining that he has only been loaned to her.

One day, two children see Matt through the window, but he is too afraid to speak to them. Celia identifies them as Steven Alacrán, a thirteen-year-old boy from the Big House, and his friend Emilia Mendoza, also thirteen, whose father is a US senator. The next day, Steven and Emilia return with Emilia's younger sister, María. Matt breaks through the window and jumps out, landing in his bare feet on the shattered glass.

Steven carries Matt, who is bleeding profusely

and in great pain, to the Big House. As Rosa, the housekeeper, and the children try to remove the glass, they discover writing on the bottom of Matt's foot: "Property of the Alacrán Estate." Just then, Steven's father comes into the room and orders that Matt, whom he calls "this little beast," be taken from the house and the sheet he is lying on be burned. Rosa dumps Matt on the lawn, where he lies alone as darkness falls. The children watch from a distance, and Steven explains that Matt is a clone of El Patrón, who is so powerful that he can protect his clones' intelligence. Clearly all the children know about clones, whom they despise as less than human. Willum, the doctor, arrives, removes the last bit of glass, and turns Matt over to an unwilling Rosa to care for. Later that night, María sneaks into Matt's room with food and sleeps curled up by his side. When she is discovered, she is sent away, and Matt is imprisoned by Rosa in a small room filled with sawdust. He lives there for six months, visited only by insects, the doctor, and Steven's younger brother, Tom, who torments Matt through the window. Finally Matt withdraws into silence. Even when María and Celia find him and call to him through his window, he does not speak.

Chapters 6–14: Middle Age: 7 to 11

One morning, Rosa cleans Matt up and takes him to meet Matteo Alacrán, the old man known as El Patrón who visits this house only occasionally. Celia is also there, and she describes Matt's poor treatment. El Patrón is angry, and Rosa is taken away. Matt and the old man take an instant liking to each other. The old man shares a fine dinner with Matt and talks about his impoverished childhood in what used to be called Mexico but is now Aztlán. People from his town were called *alacránes*, or scorpions, and when the man became rich he changed his name to Matteo Alacrán to honor them. Matt, who has the same name, is happy to share something with his new friend. Matt is returned to Celia's care in a fine apartment in the mansion. The Alacrán family is instructed to treat Matt with respect, although they continue to despise him, and El Patrón appoints a bodyguard, Tam Lin, to protect Matt.

María remains his friend, although she also spends time with Tom, who is cruel to Matt and not very nice to María. Tom can look apologetic and sincere when he has done something bad, and most people fall for his innocent looks. He and Matt hate each other. Soon vacation is over, and María and the other children go back to school. Tam Lin finds a teacher for Matt: she is a slow-witted woman who repeats the same lesson over and over. Matt becomes so frustrated that he shouts at her—the first time he has spoken in months. Tam Lin gently sends her away and eventually explains that she is an "eejit," a person whose brain has been treated so that she can perform only one task. Now that Matt is speaking again, Tam Lin decides to begin Matt's real education.

Tam Lin and Matt get a horse and ride away for a picnic. As they pass the poppy fields, they see a farm worker lying dead. Tam Lin explains that this man is also an eejit, programmed to work in the fields without stopping; the man probably did not hear the command to drink water and kept working in the heat until he died. Past the Alacrán boundary, they climb a steep mountain to a secret oasis where they can speak privately. Tam Lin wants Matt to know what a clone is, how he was created from a bit of El Patrón's flesh, that most people hate clones, and that the old man wants his clone to be brought up well.

Media Adaptations

- *The House of the Scorpion,* recorded as an unabridged audiobook and read by Broadway performer Raul Esparza, was produced by Simon & Schuster Audio in 2004.

Tam Lin and Celia arrange for Matt to study through distance learning, and he does very well. María comes to visit on holidays, bringing her dog Furball, but when he is alone, Matt explores the house. He enjoys hiding behind the plants and listening to Felicia, the mother of Steven and Tom, play the piano. Once a concert pianist, she is now a sad, lonely alcoholic whose husband ignores her. Matt discovers a series of tunnels running through the house behind the closets with peepholes into most of the rooms. Spying on the family, he overhears a strange conversation. The doctor and Mr. Alacrán (Steven's father), are trying to persuade Mr. Alacrán's sick father, called El Viejo ("the old man"), to seek treatment or a transplant.

El Patrón returns to celebrate his one hundred and forty-third birthday. All of the children come back for the party, and Tom plays a mean trick on María, hiding Furball in the toilet with the lid closed. In addition to the Alacrán and Mendoza families, important business and government leaders from around the world attend the party, including Mr. MacGregor, who runs a large Farm near San Diego. El Patrón has received fetal brain implants to give him more vitality. He and MacGregor compare health treatments and make fun of El Viejo, El Patrón's grandson, because he refuses to extend his life beyond what he believes God has given him.

All of the guests pay homage to El Patrón, bringing him expensive presents and listening to his life story, which they have heard many times. Matt, resentful that María is being nice to Tom, switches the place cards so that María will sit next to him at dinner and Tom will be at the baby table. Tam Lin quietly scolds Matt, but El Patrón praises him for dealing in this way with an enemy. El Patrón's birthday is, in a way, also Matt's, and on this day Matt can ask for anything. Still angry with María, he orders her to give him a kiss. The crowd protests —the idea of a human's kissing a clone is repulsive to them—but El Patrón insists, and no one dares go against him. Too late, Matt realizes that he is humiliating his friend, not winning her back.

The next day, Tom tricks Matt and María into meeting him in the hospital wing and shows them a deranged, sick clone of MacGregor's strapped to a bed, howling. Matt and María are upset about the suffering clone. Matt worries that as he ages he will go mad as well. Celia explains that the clone's brain was damaged when he was born and that Matt was spared this damage. She also explains that while Felicia is Tom's mother, his father is not Mr. Alacrán but Mr. MacGregor, with whom Felicia once ran off. El Patrón made her and Tom come back, but no one in the family loves or respects them. Matt still has questions: How can he gain María's forgiveness? Will his brain be damaged later? Why does MacGregor need a clone at all?

Matt decides to force María to listen to his apology by kidnapping Furball and holding him hostage until she agrees to meet with Matt. He steals a bottle of Felicia's laudanum, a sleeping drug made from opium, planning to give some to Furball to keep him quiet. When he kidnaps Furball, the dog stays quiet, so Matt does not give him the drug. The next day, Furball is found dead, killed with an overdose of laudanum from a bottle with Matt's fingerprints on it. No one, not even Tam Lin or Celia, believes that Matt did not kill the dog, and María's father, Senator Mendoza, takes the girl away. To make things even worse, Tam Lin tells Matt that El Patrón is leaving again and Tam Lin is going with him.

Chapters 15–22: Old Age: 12 to 14

Lonely with Tam Lin and María gone, Matt returns to the hidden oasis, getting a horse from Rosa, now an eejit who does not even recognize him. At the oasis, Matt finds blankets, pots, food, and books that Tam Lin has left for him with a note signed, "Yor frend." Feeling better, Matt returns to the mansion and learns that El Viejo has died. During the funeral, attended by family and friends, the priest orders that Matt be removed from the holy event. María defends Matt, and he knows he has been forgiven. Matt and María slip off to the tunnels to talk. From there, they overhear Tom and Felicia talking disrespectfully about El Viejo, and Felicia laughingly tells Tom that she killed Furball. María is shocked, but she does not have time to talk with Matt about it before Tam Lin comes to sneak her back to her father.

Matt is alone again, and returns to the oasis. He begins to read a book called *A History of Opium*, which claims that El Patrón is evil, a powerful man who became wealthy through the illegal drug trade. This is news to Matt. For his lifetime, drugs have been legal. The book explains that a hundred years before, when Mexico and the United States could not control either their borders or the drug trade, the dealers proposed that each country give up a strip of land in the middle and turn it over to the drug lords, who would guard the borders and promise not to sell drugs in Mexico or the United States. The new country in the middle, called Opium, is run by the two biggest Farmers, El Patrón and MacGregor. Matt tosses the book away, refusing to believe its story.

Matt visits the water purification plant to learn how it works. He has reasoned that El Patrón must have given him a good education because he intends Matt to help run the Farm one day. Matt sees long rows of buildings with bars and small windows, where the eejit farm-workers live, and is nearly killed by the fumes from the chemical holding tanks nearby. He is rescued by two Farm Patrol guards, who become friendly when they learn who Matt is. They tell him that Tam Lin was once an activist fighting for Scottish nationalism and that, in attempting to bomb the British prime minister, he accidentally blew up a bus full of schoolchildren.

The next day, Matt is summoned to see El Patrón, who has had a heart attack. The old man receives a piggyback heart transplant, a small heart that will work in concert with his own. But it becomes clear that the small heart will not be enough. Tam Lin and Celia argue about how much Matt should know, and finally Matt realizes that he was created to provide spare parts for El Patrón. Overwhelmed by all his new knowledge, Matt returns to the oasis and uncovers one more secret: *The History of Opium* was written by Esperanza Mendoza, the mother María thought had died years ago.

El Patrón stabilizes, and again the house is busy, this time with the wedding of Steven and Emilia. MacGregor arrives looking young and healthy, and María arrives looking happy and beautiful. María reveals that she knows Matt's fate and that she is expected to marry Tom when they are old enough, and Matt tells María that her mother seems to be alive. Matt is not invited to the wedding, but he watches it from one of the peepholes. When El Patrón has another heart attack, everyone looks for Matt so they can use his heart for a transplant. María tries to help him escape, but he is caught and taken to the hospital.

Chapters 23–25: Age 14

Matt is brought to El Patrón, who wonders why Matt, like the clones before him, does not appreciate that he has been given fourteen years of life and education. But when it is time to prepare Matt for surgery, Celia announces that she has been giving him low doses of arsenic for months, making his organs unfit for transplant. El Patrón dies. Tam Lin offers to "dispose of the clone" but instead takes

Matt to the oasis and helps him pack up to escape to Aztlán, where he will be able to find María at school. Back at the mansion, Celia was to be turned into an eejit, but she is only pretending to be one. Tam Lin says goodbye to Matt for the last time. Matt hikes over the mountains, evades the Farm Patrol, and literally falls over the border into Aztlán.

Chapters 26–38: La Vida Nueva

Matt is picked up by two border guards, who take him to an orphanage. There, for the first time, he is surrounded by other children who treat him as an equal. The orphanage is staffed by Keepers who make the boys work endlessly and feed them nothing but plankton. They indoctrinate the boys to make them docile, having them recite the Five Principles of Good Citizenship and the Four Attitudes Leading to Right-Mindedness over and over. The orphans are from Aztlán, captured when they were trying to cross the border into Opium with their parents. Many boys believe that their parents have found better lives across the border, and Matt does not tell them that they were probably caught and turned into eejits. Matt becomes friends with the tough, cynical Chacho and Fidelito, a small, sickly boy. All three boys are transferred to a plankton-processing plant near San Luis, the city where María's convent is.

The Keepers at the plankton factory are cruel to the boys. In the evenings, the boys are supposed to confess transgressions, but Matt does not believe he has done anything wrong and stays quiet. A new friend is Ton-Ton, an older boy. He appears to be unintelligent, but Matt can see that Ton-Ton is just a slow, deliberate thinker. One night, Ton-Ton is punished for a small offense by being beaten with a cane until he is bloody. Matt is also hit a few times, and when he does not cry out, the other boys admire his bravery. But when he still does not seem to accept his position and the Keepers' teachings, they turn on Fidelito as a last attempt to break Matt's will. Jorge, a Keeper, tries to beat Fidelito with the cane. Matt knows the beating could kill the smaller boy, and he and Chacho attack Jorge and hold him down. The Keepers break up the fight, and Jorge taunts the boys by revealing that Matt is a clone, or *crot*, and calling Ton-Ton stupid.

That night, Jorge orders Matt's and Chachós mouths, wrists, and ankles bound with tape and has them tossed into a massive pit filled with bones. The boys manage to escape, and they are picked up by Ton-Ton and Fidelito, who are driving a shrimp harvester. The boys have staged a mutiny, locked the Keepers in their rooms, and dosed them with enough laudanum to keep them asleep for a long time. After Ton-Ton drives the large machine to the fence and uses its claws to tear a hole in it, the boys escape into San Luis and make their way to the Convent of Santa Clara. Chacho has been seriously injured, and the sisters care for him in their hospital. Jorge and the other Keepers show up and try to take the four escapees back, but they are stopped by the strong, sharp-tongued woman in charge, Doña Esperanza—María's mother. María appears and greets Matt with an excited hug.

Esperanza has been trying for years to bring down the drug lords and free the eejits. Now she is especially concerned because Opium has been under a lockdown for months, with no one allowed in or out. Esperanza hopes that Matt, an exact copy of El Patrón. will be able to use his fingerprints and DNA code to get through Opium's elaborate security system. She asks him to try, although it could be dangerous, and tells him that according to international law Matt is now the only El Patrón, the head of the drug business and the owner of everything the old man owned. Matt sneaks into Opium and returns to the mansion. He reunites with Celia, who tells him a horrible story: at El Patrón's funeral, the guests went down to the vaults where the dead man kept his treasure and, according to his wishes, drank a toast with special wine he had saved. Nearly all of the guests, including Tam Lin, died. Matt rides to the oasis and begins to plan how he will repurpose his poppy fields for food crops and bring in doctors to reverse the damage to the eejits. He knows that he will succeed, with the help of Celia and María and his friends from Aztlán.

Characters

Felicia Alacrán

Felicia is the wife of Mr. Alacrán and the mother of Steven, Tom, and an older son named Benito. Before her marriage, she was a concert pianist, and she still plays beautifully. However, no one listens to her play; she spends most of her time alone, ignored by her family. Felicia, like all of the Alacrán family, is under the thumb of El Patrón. Years before the novel begins, Felicia had an affair with Mr. MacGregor and went to live with him, bearing him a son, Tom. But El Patrón, who does not willingly give up anything—or anyone—made them come back, and now Felicia lives in a home where no one wants her. She drinks heavily and also takes laudanum, a drug that helps her sleep. Felicia feels powerless, but she is protective of Tom and resentful of the attention Matt gets. To get back at the family for their bad treatment of Tom at El Patrón's birthday party, she kills María's dog Furball and lets Matt take the blame. Months later, Matt and María overhear Felicia telling Tom that she killed the dog, and they also discover that she has been spying on the family with the cameras set up through the house.

Matteo Alacrán

See El Patrón

Mr. Alacrán

Mr. Alacrán is the father of Steven and another son, the son of El Viejo, and the great-grandson of El Patrón. When El Patrón is away, Mr. Alacrán is the master of the Big House, but El Patrón makes all the important decisions. His first action in the novel is to enter the room where five-year-old Matt has been brought because of his bleeding foot. Mr. Alacrán recognizes Matt as a clone and orders him out of the house. Like most people, he hates clones, and he is cordial to Matt only because El Patrón has ordered it. Mr. Alacrán was humiliated years ago when his wife, Felicia, ran off with Mr. MacGregor, and his humiliation was compounded when El Patrón ordered that Felicia and her illegitimate son, Tom, come back to the mansion to live. Mr. Alacrán completely ignores Felicia and sends Tom to boarding school. His only tenderness is for his father, El Viejo. He pleads with his father to extend his life with transplants from clones, but El Viejo refuses and Mr. Alacrán is genuinely saddened when his father dies.

Steven Alacrán

Steven is the son of Felicia and Mr. Alacrán, the grandson of El Viejo, and the great-great-grandson of El Patrón. He is thirteen years old when he and his friend Emilia discover five-year-old Matt living in a small house in the poppy fields. When Matt jumps out of the window and cuts his foot, Steven carries him to the Big House, not yet realizing that Matt is a clone. When Matt's identity is revealed, Steven explains to the younger children what clones are and why Matt's brain was not damaged when he was born. Steven is away at school most of the year, and when he is home, he generally ignores Matt but does not actively try to hurt him. When he is old enough, it is arranged that he is to marry Emilia to solidify the bonds between the two important drug families; fortunately, the two like each other. It is during their wedding that El Patrón suffers his last heart attack. María tries to help Matt escape, but she is stopped by Steven and Emilia; Steven declares that Matt is the same as livestock and turns him over to the bodyguards.

Tom Alacrán

Red-haired Tom lives as the youngest son of the Alacrán family, but he is really the son of Felicia and Mr. MacGregor. El Patrón wants Tom in his house when the boy is not at school, but he speaks openly about how he does not like Tom. In fact, there is little to like. Tom is cruel to Matt, taunting him through the bars of his prison when Matt is under Rosa's care and relentlessly pointing out that Matt, as a clone, is not human and not worthy of the most basic respect. Tom is even unkind to María, playing little tricks on her, such as hiding Furball in the toilet with the lid closed and then pretending to help look for him. As Matt observes, Tom has mastered looking innocent and sincere when he is neither. Shortly after the birthday party, when Matt humiliates Tom by sending him to the baby table, Tom tricks Matt and María into going to the hospital wing of the mansion and shows them a howling, insane clone of Mr. MacGregor; he tells them that soon Matt will also become insane. The hospital and the clone were supposed to be a secret, so Tom is sent to a year-round boarding school as punishment. When the children come back for Emilia and Steven's wedding, María tells Matt that she is expected to marry Tom one day and that she does not mind; she believes that with love and patience she can change him, while Matt continues to believe that Tom is evil. But when Matt learns that Tom has died with the other funeral guests, he realizes that "Tom had been no more in charge of his fate than the dullest eejit."

Celia

Celia is a cook in the Big House and is the woman charged with raising Matt from babyhood. She and Matt live alone in a small house surrounded by poppies, and she loves and protects him, knowing that he is a clone and will live only until his organs are needed to save El Patrón's life. She forbids Matt to call her *Mamá*; she tells Matt that he has only been loaned to her but does not explain until he is much older what his fate is to be. After Matt is taken to the Big House at the age of five, he is taken from Celiás care for several months, but then she and Matt are given an apartment in the mansion and Celia and Tam Lin act as his surrogate parents. When Matt is fourteen and El Patrón has his first heart attack, Celia begins slowly poisoning Matt so his organs will not be fit for transplanting. Her trick is revealed, and she is sent to work in the stables; she is supposed to be turned into an eejit, but Tam Lin only marks her forehead to make it look as though her brain has been interfered with. Matt does not see her again until the novel's end, when he finds her in the mansion. As a mere servant, Celia was not with the family when they all died at El Patrón's funeral. Matt knows he can count on her love and wisdom to help him rebuild the land of Opium.

Chacho

Chacho is one of the boys Matt meets in the orphanage at the Aztlán border. He is tough, with big hands and dark hair. He is a skilled woodworker and is making himself a guitar from a scrap of wood until it is taken away from him because orphans are not allowed to have hobbies. Chacho is the only one of the orphans who dares to say out loud that he hates the Keepers, and he warns Matt from the beginning that life in the orphanage will be difficult. Chacho believes that his father is wealthy and living in the United States, waiting only until he owns a home before he sends for Chacho, but Matt is sure that Chacho's father, like all the others who have tried to get across the border, was caught and made an eejit. Chacho is sent to the plankton factory in San Luis with Fidelito and Matt, and he gradually comes to respect Matt and protect Fidelito, though he avoids showing any emotion. When Matt attacks

Jorge to keep him from beating Fidelito, Chacho joins him, and the two are bound and thrown into the boneyard to die. Chacho is seriously injured, and when the boys manage to get him out, he is weak and in terrible pain. Once the boys make their way to San Luis, Chacho is taken to be cared for to the hospital at the Convent of Santa Clara.

The Doctor

The doctor, whose first name is Willum, is the personal physician to the Alacrán family, charged with keeping El Patrón alive and with keeping Matt healthy until his organs are needed for transplants.

El Patrón

El Patrón, whose title means "the boss" or "the landlord," is the head of the Alacrán family and the biggest drug lord and most powerful person in the land known as Opium. His overwhelming bitterness is traced to his childhood: he lived in extreme poverty and was the only one of nine siblings to live to adulthood. His legal name is Matteo Alacrán, but this is a name he gave himself when he started to become successful; *alacrán* is the Spanish word for "scorpion," and the poor common people of the small village where he grew up were called *alacránes* by others who looked down on them. El Patrón is ruthless and heartless. He has no affection for his family and friends, no consideration for others, and no regard for human life. People fear and obey him, and he controls his family even so far as dictating where they live and whom they marry. His poppy fields are tended by eejits, or people whose brains have been manipulated so they work tirelessly and make no demands.

When the novel opens, El Patrón is nearly one hundred and forty years old, having extended his life by having clones created and then harvesting their tissues and organs whenever one of his own parts begins to fail. Many wealthy people use clones this way, but El Patrón is unusual in insisting that his clones' intelligence be preserved when they are harvested. He wants them to have the comfort and education that he did not have as a child, and he does not understand why they are not grateful for their privileged lives when it is time for them to die.

For a time, Matt admires El Patrón and enjoys being under his protection. He can see that the older man is cruel but also that he is successful. When Matt is fourteen years old, El Patrón suffers a series of heart attacks, and Matt finally understands that his own heart is required for a transplant. However, Celia has been gradually poisoning Matt so his heart cannot be used, and El Patrón dies. Even at his funeral, held while Matt is escaping, everyone follows the orders El Patrón has left behind. They carry his jewel-encrusted coffin down into the catacombs where he has been stockpiling treasure for years, and they drink a toast with special wine that El Patrón has set aside for this day. The wine is poisoned, and nearly everyone in attendance—El Patrón's family, competitors, bodyguards, and colleagues—dies.

El Viejo

El Viejo is the father of Mr. Alacrán and the grandson of El Patrón. Everyone calls him "El Viejo," the old man, because he is old and sick. Unlike El Patrón and Mr. MacGregor, he refuses to be cloned and have treatments that will keep him young and healthy. Instead he insists that he is ready to accept only the years of life that God gives him. When El Viejo dies, many in the family mock him for not fighting death, but Mr. Alacrán grieves.

Fidelito

Fidelito, about eight years old, is a small, skinny orphan who misses his *abuelita*, or grandmother, and is desperate for approval. He looks up to Matt, and Matt takes him under his wing, helping him reach his work quota each day and making sure he gets enough food. With Matt and Chacho, Fidelito is transferred to the plankton factory in San Luis. When Jorge, one of the Keepers there, notices that Fidelito idolizes Matt, he begins tormenting Fidelito to punish Matt. Finally, Jorge attempts to beat Fidelito with his cane, and Matt and Chacho stop the beating by attacking Jorge. When they are thrown into the boneyard to die, Fidelito and Ton-Ton come to their rescue with a large shrimp-harvesting vehicle, and the four boys escape into San Luis.

Furball

Furball is María's little dog. María carries the dog everywhere, kisses it, and talks to it. Others do not treat Furball so nicely: Tom hides him in the toilet with the lid down, and Felicia kills the dog and allows Matt to take the blame.

Jorge

Jorge is one of the Keepers assigned to watch over the boys at the plankton factory outside San Luis. He is cruel to the boys under his charge, delighting in bringing them under his control. Unable to break Matt's spirit and get him to accept the wisdom of the Five Principles of Good Citizenship and the Four Attitudes Leading to Right-Mindfulness, Jorge tells the rest of the boys that Matt is an escaped *crot*, or a zombie from Opium. He starts picking on small, frail Fidelito as a way to bring Matt in line. When Jorge's taunts and threats are about to turn to physical violence, Matt attacks him to protect Fidelito. Jorge orders Matt and Chacho, who joined in the attack, to be bound with tape, tossed into the boneyard, and left to die. That night, while Matt and Chacho struggle, Ton-Ton gives Jorge and the other Keepers enough laudanum to knock them out and barricades their compound. Jorge shows up again later, at Chacho's bedside in the hospital at the Convent of Santa Clara, but instead of taking the boys back to the factory, Jorge is arrested on charges of dealing drugs.

Mr. MacGregor

Mr. MacGregor is an old friend and competitor of El Patrón's, the owner of the second-largest drug Farm in Opium. The two men share talk of business and swap stories about how they have extended their lives using transplants from clones. MacGregor is also the father of Felicia's son Tom; she ran off with him for a time but returned to the Alacrán home with Tom under orders from El Patrón. This transgression does not seem to have affected the relationship between Mr. MacGregor and El Patrón, but neither man shows any affection or respect for either Felicia or Tom.

Matt

Matt, the protagonist, is just an embryo when he is introduced and fourteen years old when the novel ends. He is a clone of the drug lord El Patrón, created in a laboratory and gestated in a cow. Unlike other clones, Matt does not have his brain damaged when he is harvested; El Patrón likes to have his clones' intelligence spared. What Matt does not understand until much later is that he was created to provide spare parts; whenever El Patrón requires replacement of a major organ, it will come from Matt. Until that time, Matt lives under the care of Celia. For his first five years, he and Celia live alone in a small house out in the poppy fields. When he comes to the mansion for the first time, Matt learns that he is a clone and that he has not had any companions because clones are despised by humans, who do not even want to touch fabric that he has touched.

Matt meets El Patrón when he is five. He is attracted to El Patrón, who seems to like him, too, but Matt does not understand their relationship. As he grows older, he sees that the rest of the Alacráns hate and fear the old man. Matt befriends María Mendoza, and she, Celia, and the bodyguard Tam Lin are the only people who treat Matt with affection. When Matt is fourteen, El Patrón suffers a series of heart attacks, and Matt comes to understand what everyone else has always known: he will now be killed and his heart transplanted into the old man. Matt escapes to a secret oasis in the desert, where Tam Lin has left equipment and maps for him to sneak across the border into Aztlán.

When Matt gets away from the Farm, he lands in an orphanage with other boys, most of whom lost their parents while trying to get across the border, through Opium, and into the United States. Matt makes new friends—Chacho, Fidelito, and Ton-Ton —and helps them escape the cruel treatment of the orphanage. They make their way to San Luis, where Matt reunites with María. Soon he is sent back to the Farm and discovers that El Patrón and his colleagues and family members are dead. As the only surviving Matteo Alacrán—as the new El Patrón—Matt begins to plan a new future of peace and justice for the Farm.

Emilia Mendoza

Emilia, the older sister of María, is the first of the children to see Matt through the window of the little house he shares with Celia. She is thirteen years old at the time, with pretty dark hair and eyes, and Matt likes her right away. In the following years, after Matt's identity is revealed, she generally ignores him rather than outwardly showing any distaste, and Matt thinks of her as relatively kind. When she and Steven are about twenty-two, they are ordered to marry to solidify the bonds between the Alacrán and Mendoza families; fortunately, the two like each other and are happy to be wed. During the wedding, however, El Patrón suffers a serious heart attack, and in the ensuing hunt for Matt, Emilia shows her true nature by stopping Matt from escaping with María and turning him over to the bodyguards. She also reveals that, unlike María, she has known all along that their mother is alive and that she has no respect for either María or Esperanza, their mother, because they have too much sympathy for clones and eejits.

Esperanza Mendoza

Esperanza is the long-lost mother of María and Emilia. She left home when María was five years old, and the girl has always assumed that her mother was dead. Instead Esperanza left her family to escape the evil dealings of her husband, Senator Mendoza, who is a close ally of El Patrón, and she has been working from outside Opium to unseat the drug lords. Esperanza helped start a group called the Anti-Slavery Society of California, dedicated to freeing the eejits, and wrote the book *The History of Opium* that Tam Lin leaves for Matt. She also won the Nobel Peace Prize. When Matt gets to the Convent of Santa Clara to see Chacho, he finds Esperanza there, reunited with María. Esperanza explains to Matt that under international law he is now the only Matteo Alacrán, and she persuades him to return to Opium and undo the harm that El Patrón created.

María Mendoza

María, about the same age as Matt, is the younger sister of Emilia and the daughter of Senator Mendoza; as far as she knows through most of the novel, her mother, Esperanza, died when María was five. When María first sees Matt through the window, she invites him to play. She never believes the bad things the others say about clones, and she takes care of Matt and pets him the same way she treats her dog, Furball. María is Matt's only friend. The two are together whenever María visits the Alacrán house, but she also is friendly with Tom, who constantly teases her. Matt and Tom are rivals for María's affection. At El Patrón's birthday party, Matt orders María to kiss him in front of the guests. María obeys, but she is humiliated and angry. To win her forgiveness, Matt makes a plan to kidnap Furball and hold him hostage until María listens to his apology, but the plan goes horribly wrong and Furball is killed. No one will believe that Matt did not kill the dog, and the rift between the friends grows deeper.

María is sent to a convent school and returns ready to forgive. When El Viejo dies and Matt is ordered away from the funeral by the priest, María speaks out in Matt's defense. The two escape into the hidden tunnels to talk privately, and they overhear Felicia telling Tom that it was she who killed Furball, letting Matt take the blame. María and Matt next meet at the wedding of Steven and Emilia. El Patrón has a serious heart attack, the bodyguards look for Matt to use his heart for a transplant, and once again Matt and María hide in the tunnels. This time Matt tells María that Esperanza, her mother, is still alive, and María reveals that she has known for some time what Matt's fate was to be. She also indicates that she expects to marry Tom when they are old enough and that she does not mind. She tries to sneak Matt to safety in her hovercraft, but they are stopped by Steven and Emilia, and Matt is taken away.

When Matt escapes from the Farm and then from the plankton factory, it is with the hope that he can reach the Convent of Santa Clara in San Luis and find María there. Eventually he does reach the convent and finds not only María but Esperanza as well. María greets Matt with an excited hug.

Senator Mendoza

Senator Mendoza is the father of Emilia and María, husband of Esperanza, and a close friend of El Patrón. He is also a US senator. Mendoza is a frequent visitor to the Alacrán mansion and sends his daughters there during school vacations. He does not like María to spend time with Matt and is particularly enraged when, during El Patrón's birthday party, Matt orders María to kiss him in front of the guests. He takes María away, vowing she will never see Matt again. After that, when María returns to the house for a funeral or a wedding, she and Matt have to meet in secret. Late in the novel, when Esperanza tells Matt that Opium has been under a lockdown for months, she chides María for worrying about her father, "an evil man." In fact, Senator Mendoza has died along with the other mourners at El Patrón's funeral.

Rosa

At the beginning of the novel, Rosa is the housekeeper in the Alacrán mansion. When Matt is handed over to her for safekeeping, she resents having to be near a clone and treats him cruelly. She gives him only enough food to keep him alive and makes him live in a room filled with sawdust so she will not have to clean up after him. When El Patrón learns how she has cared for Matt, he has her sent out of the house. She is turned into an eejit and given a job in the stables.

Tam Lin

Tam Lin is one of El Patrón's bodyguards, assigned to protect Matt. Tam Lin is loyal to El Patrón, but he becomes a father figure to Matt and tries to protect him. Tam Lin takes Matt to a hidden oasis in the desert where they will not be overheard, and there he talks to Matt about responsibility and honor and teaches him to climb mountains and survive in the desert. Tam Lin is Matt's moral guide: he tries to keep Matt from demanding a kiss from María at the birthday party and expresses his disappointment when Matt will not confess to killing Furball. Tam Lin leaves the mansion to accompany El Patrón, but he leaves survival gear and food for Matt in the oasis, as well as a book about El Patrón's ascendancy to power. When Celia begins to poison Matt to make his organs unfit for transplanting, Tam Lin tries to talk her out of it, but he stands by her and protects her when she is found out: he has her sent to work in the stables and marks her forehead so it looks as though she has had her brain damaged. When Matt finally escapes from the Farm, he does it with the training and the equipment Tam Lin has given him. But Tam Lin does not escape. Before working for El Patrón, he was a political activist in Scotland, where, trying to assassinate the prime minister, he accidentally killed twenty schoolchildren. Accepting that he deserves to be punished, Tam Lin knowingly drinks the poisoned wine with the others at El Patrón's funeral.

The Teacher

The teacher is a woman whose brain has been intentionally damaged—an eejit. She comes to the Big House to be Matt's tutor after El Patrón orders that Matt be educated, but she has been programmed to deliver only one very simple lesson over and over. Matt is so frustrated with her that he breaks his months-long silence to shout at her.

Ton-Ton

Ton-Ton is one of the boys at the plankton factory near San Luis. A bit older, he has the responsibility of driving the big shrimp harvester and of cleaning the Keepers' rooms. He is loyal to the Keepers even when he is beaten because they rescued him from the Farm Patrol. Ton-Ton is a slow thinker, but a deep thinker. When Jorge calls Ton-Ton stupid, Ton-Ton realizes that the Keepers have never respected or cared for him. And when Matt and Chacho are tossed into the boneyard, Ton-Ton drugs the Keepers with laudanum, and he and Fidelito take the shrimp-harvester to rescue the boys. As the four work their way toward the Convent of Santa Clara, Ton-Ton figures out how to break through the fence, knows how to treat Chacho's injuries, and gives Matt and Fidelito last-minute advice about how to get to get to town.

Willum

See The Doctor

Themes

Identity

The central questions facing Matt throughout the novel are questions of identity: Who and what is he? Is he a *him* or an *it*? As a clone, harvested rather than born of a mother, is he truly less than human, incapable of the human decency that almost no one expects him to demonstrate? Does he have a right to live a full life—a basic human right—or must he willingly accept that when his time comes, he must sacrifice his own body to save El Patrón?

In the beginning, Matt does not know he is different, and when the Alacráns identify him as a clone and have him thrown out of the Big House, he does not understand why they think he is "a little beast" and "a bad animal." Gradually he learns what a clone is and accepts the view that he is like an animal; when María tries to get him to talk, he snaps at her, thinking, "Being a clone was bad no matter what you did, so why bother being good at all?" He observes that Tom is often punished for teasing María, while Matt is never punished. To Matt, this means that no one thinks him capable of learning right from wrong, that he and the dog, Furball, are "both animals and thus unimportant." Even when Matt's life is going relatively well, when he is doing well at his studies and enjoying playing music, he is dragged down emotionally by his status: "He understood he was only a photograph of a human, and that meant he wasn't really important."

Celia and Tam Lin, however, always treat Matt as though he is valuable and teachable. Celia cherishes him and vows to protect him, and she shields him as long as she can from the hurtful knowledge that he is a clone. Tam Lin teaches Matt the values and qualities that will make him a man of character. Matt has flashes of understanding that he is not simply a copy. For example, he is a talented musician, although El Patrón, as Felicia puts it, "doesn't have a… musical bone in his body." That talent, Matt senses, is his own, is Matt. Still, he horribly misunderstands his relationship with El Patrón, thinking he "could read and write, climb hills, play music, and do anything a real human might do—all because El Patrón loved him." He resolves that "if he wasn't human, he might become something even better."

Like many young men, Matt does not fully come into his own identity until he is separated from his home and family and is out on his own. Only when El Patrón reveals his real plans for Matt (plans that all the other characters—as well as the reader—have understood well before Matt does) and then dies, only when Matt has crossed the desert and faced emotional and physical dangers in Aztlán, only when he has relied on himself, can he know who he really is. And so he is ready to receive the truth when Esperanza Mendoza gives it to him: with El Patrôn dead he *is* El Patrón. "You have his body and his identity," she says. When María asks whether Matt is human, Esperanza replies clearly, "He always was."

Topics for Further Study

- Novelists have long been interested in exploring what happens to children when they are separated from their families and placed under harsh control. What qualities of Matt's character help him survive and build community in the orphanage and the plankton factory in *The House of the Scorpion*? Compare Matt's qualities with those that shape the fate of any of the young men in William Golding's *Lord of the Flies* or characters from other novels. With a few classmates, stage a panel discussion or create a blog, with each member taking on the role of a different character explaining how she or he thrived or the mistakes she or he made. Invite classmates to ask questions or make comments.

- Using information gleaned from the novel, as well as information from Farmer's "Author's Note" and any interviews you can find with the author, draw a map that includes the land of Opium, the oasis, the Farms of El Patrón and Mr. MacGregor, the Convent of San Luis, the boneyard, and other landmarks. With your classmates, trace Matt's journey of escape on your map.

- Read a few other stories that feature dragon hoards. You might consider *The Hobbit* by J. R. R. Tolkien, *The Dragon Hoard* by Tanith Lee, *Beowulf*, or any number of Scandinavian folk tales. Or you might turn to the "Dragon Hoard" board games, card games, online games, or video games. Write a paper in which you explore how Farmer retained some common qualities of dragon hoard stories while changing others when she set her own dragon hoard beneath a future Arizona desert.

- The eejits in *The House of the*

Scorpion work in terrible conditions with no ability to ask for more. Learn what you can about the workers who harvest crops in the American Southwest today. Put together a presentation for your class, showing the working and living conditions of these workers.

- Consider the positions of El Viejo, the old man who refuses to accept extreme treatments to extend his life, and of Mr. Alacrán, who does not wish to see his father die. Write a short play or screenplay showing a debate between the two men. Incorporate dialogue from the novel if you like, but give the debate a fuller treatment to more completely articulate their beliefs.

- El Patrón's chief crop is opium poppies, used to make heroin. Research the production of heroin today and write a paper explaining what you learn. Where is most of the drug produced? How does it get into the United States? What efforts is the United States engaged in to combat heroin production and distribution?

Family

Just as Matt tries to figure out what it means to be human, he has to learn what a family is. For the first five years of his life, he lives with Celia in what seems to be a normal, loving, single-parent family. However, Celia does not allow Matt to call her *Mamá*, a name he has heard on television, because he is not her child but only "loaned" to her. Of course, Matt learns later that does not have a mother and was not even gestated in a woman's body. As a clone, he feels that he has no family at all.

The families he observes, on the other hand, are nothing to envy. The Alacráns are bitter and fearful, ruled over by El Patrón, the great-great-grandfather of María who refuses to die, refuses to share power, refuses to let his descendants make their own decisions. El Patrón himself had an unhappy family life; none of his five brothers and three sisters lived long enough to start their own families. The only married couples who appear in the novel are Mr. Alacrán and Felicia, who hate each other, and the sons of Mr. Alacrán, who had their wives chosen for them by El Patrón to further his business interests. Senator and Esperanza Mendoza do not live together; in fact, Esperanza left the family when María was five years old, and she refers to the Senator as "an evil man." Felicia and Mr. MacGregor are Tom's parents, but MacGregor does not acknowledge Tom on the rare occasions he sees him. Tom spends most of his time away at boarding schools, or at the mansion with his sad, alcoholic mother. Tom is insufferably cruel and dull, but even Matt comes to see at the end that "Tom had been no more in control of his fate than the dullest eejit." The orphans in Aztlán are all separated from their families, and though they dream of reuniting with them one day across the border, Matt knows that the parents are in truth dead or turned to eejits.

The only happy, loving family in the novel is the family of Matt, Celia, and Tam Lin. Scenes of the three of them together in their wing of the mansion, telling stories or celebrating Matt's birthday, seem like normal family moments, although they are bound not by blood but only by love. Celia and Tam Lin have no other family, either, but their love for each other and for Matt is clear. But because Matt does not recognize his own humanity, he does not recognize that he is living in a family. When he is escaping with the other boys, however, and he mentions Celia's name, he suddenly realizes that Celia is, in every important way, his mother. "No one else cared for him the way she did. No one protected him or loved him so much, except, perhaps, Tam Lin. And Tam Lin was like his father." Only when Matt is away from the poisonous atmosphere of El Patrón's mansion can he understand what a real family is. By the end of the novel, there are hints that he and María, who is now under the influence of her own mother, will be able to form a new family of their own as they create a new future for Opium.

Third-person Point of View

The point of view of *The House of the Scorpion*, or the way in which the narrator looks at the action and "speaks" to the reader, is called "third person limited." It is third person because the narrative voice is not one of the characters, but uses *he* and *she* and *they* to refer to them. In other words, the narrator of the story is not part of the story but an observer. The point of view is limited because the narrator cannot see equally into the feelings and thoughts of all the characters but only into Matt's. This creates an interesting experience for the reader because, especially early on in the novel, when Matt is still quite young, the reader understands things about Matt's situation that Matt does not. For example, as a toddler, Matt does not realize that living alone with Celia out in the middle of poppy fields is strange; to him, it is normal, but the reader immediately senses that something is not right. When Matt and the reader overhear Celia and Tam Lin arguing about how much Matt should be told, the reader understands already that Matt is a clone destined for death, but Matt does not. And when Matt thinks to himself that he can "read and write, climb hills, play music, and do anything a real human might do—all because El Patrón loved him," the reader is already aware that El Patrón is incapable of love and certainly feels none for Matt.

Because of the third-person limited point of view, the reader knows things that Matt does not, and this tension elevates the *pathos*—the deep feelings of pity and affection—that the reader feels for him.

Science Fiction

Science fiction is a label given to works of fiction that are on most levels completely believable but that accept as true certain scientific ideas or inventions that do not exist in the real world. These stories are often set in the future or on faraway planets, when and where these new rules of science are plausible. The characters behave as characters would in more realistic stories, so it can be easy for readers to forget that the world these characters inhabit is imaginary. *The House of the Scorpion* is a work of science fiction, set in a future world of new technology, and yet the feelings and actions of Matt, Celia, María, and the others make perfect sense because the rules established within the world of the novel are consistent and clear.

The House of the Scorpion takes place in the future, after Mexico and the United States have each given away territory to the new world of Opium and Mexico has changed its name to Aztlán. In many ways, Opium resembles the southwestern United States of the early twenty-first century, but there are important underlying differences. The ability to clone humans and gestate them in cows is highly advanced, and a scene of a technician nurturing the group of embryos that will produce Matt is the opening scene of the novel. These clones can be used to grow replacement organs for wealthy men, and the ability to alter the clones' brains at harvest is also well developed. It is also taken for granted—at least in Opium—that people and horses can be turned into docile worker drones called eejits by the manipulation of their brains. But aside from these differences, which do not have much effect on the daily life of a child in the Big House, and the fact that visitors come and go on hovercraft, Matt's world is similar to that of the readers. As a young child, he drinks lemon soda, watches Westerns on television, and reads stories about Peter Rabbit. When he is older, he plays the piano and the guitar, studies, and loads the dishwasher.

When he prepares to leave Opium, however, Matt learns that he has been living in a deliberately old-fashioned world. El Patrón, as Tam Lin hurriedly explains, "has kept Opium from one hundred years in the past." El Patrón never arrives in a hovercraft but instead rides in a big limousine —only because he is too frail to ride a horse. Celia cooks over a wood-burning stove when El Patrón visits, but "at other times she was allowed to use microwaves." The mansion is usually cooled by breezes and roof overhangs during most of the year, using air-conditioning in the desert heat only when there are important guests to impress. Even the TV shows Matt used to watch are hundred-year-old shows broadcast under El Patrón's control. And of course, as Tam Lin points out, "the fields are harvested by people, not machines. Even rockets aren't allowed to fly over." (Tellingly, Matt does not respond in surprise to the mention of rockets.) As Matt ventures off into Aztlán and then returns to Opium as the new El Patrón, he will have to learn to use the new technologies, but as in most works of science fiction, he will be surrounded by people who feel and behave in entirely human ways.

Historical Context

Illegal Immigration

According to *A History of Opium*, the history of El Patrón and his colleagues written by Esperanza Mendoza, the country of Opium was formed when the drug dealers "approached the leaders of the United States and Mexico. 'You have two problems,' [El Patrón] said. 'First, you cannot control your borders.'" Matt remembers hearing that, when Celia was young, when Aztlín was still called Mexico, "many thousands of Mexicans had flooded across the border in search of work." Because the two countries had failed to stop illegal immigration, they allowed the creation of Opium with the understanding that the drug lords would do it for them. In 2002, when *The House of the Scorpion* was published, illegal immigration—particularly from Mexico into the United States—was an important topic for politicians and policy makers, as it continued to be for at least a decade afterward.

Mark Krikorian of the Center for Immigration studies reports in a 2012 article appearing in *National Interest* that between 2000 and 2005 approximately 850,000 illegal immigrants entered the United States each year. The most common way they entered, he writes, was by crossing the border illegally, although many simply overstayed visas that had allowed them to enter legally. In the novel, people who are caught trying to cross the border into Opium and then on to the United States are rounded up and turned into eejits who will work in the poppy fields for the rest of their lives. According to Esperanza's book, the creation of eejits is a new phenomenon, developed after even El Patrón and the others found it difficult to control the illegals: "They slipped through his fingers. They helped one another escape. The flooded across Opium to the border of the United States until that government threatened to put El Patrón out of business." In the real world, Krikorian reports that more than one million people were arrested on the border between the United States and Mexico every year from the early 1980s to 2005. The Border Patrol prevented these people from entering the United States and sent many back to their hometowns.

After about 2005, the number of immigrants illegally crossing the border between the United States and Mexico began to decline, along with the number of arrests made by the Border Patrol. In the summer of 2012, a study by Princeton University's Mexican Migration Project reported that with decreased illegal immigration, coupled with increased deportation of illegal immigrants and an increase in immigrants choosing to return home to Mexico, "the net immigration traffic had dropped to zero for the first time in 60 years," as reported in an article by Scott Zhuge in the *Harvard International Review*. However, immigration policy continued to be an important topic for debate, reaching even into the presidential campaigns of 2012.

Drug Traffic

The second problem addressed by the creation of Opium, according to Esperanza Mendoza's *A History of Opium*, was drug traffic. As El Patrón pointed out to the leaders of the United States and Mexico, "You have two problems.... First, you cannot control your borders, and second, you cannot control us." As part of the agreement that created the land of Opium, the drug lords were free to conduct their business as long as they promised "not to sell drugs to the citizens of the United States and Mexico. They would peddle their wares in Europe, Asia, and Africa instead." Thus El Patrón grows vast fields of opium poppies—the plant used to make heroin—and becomes rich and powerful. The drug lords themselves seem to live and work harmoniously, ruled by El Patrón and governed also by a council that "dealt with international problems and kept peace between the various Farms."

At the time *The House of the Scorpion* was published in 2002, there was an active drug trade that relied on a steady supply of drugs—particularly cocaine and marijuana—smuggled over the border between the United States and Mexico. International drug trafficking groups, sometimes called cartels, ran the trade from headquarters in Colombia, El Salvador, and Mexico, the drugs needed to cross the border to reach their customers in the United States. In a 2007 report to Congress, Colleen W. Cook stated that "Mexican drug cartels now dominate the wholesale illicit drug market in the United States." She reported that 90 percent of the cocaine entering the United States came across the border with Mexico and that a large portion of the heroin entering the United States also came from Mexico, although Mexico did not produce much of it. Mexico was also said to be "the main foreign supplier of marijuana and a major supplier of methamphetamine to the United States." Many lives, and many millions of dollars, were lost each year to the drug trade. The governments of the United States and Mexico were indeed at a loss for how to control drug trafficking.

Critical Overview

Considering that *The House of the Scorpion* earned so many awards when it was published—the National Book Award for Young People's Literature, Germany's prestigious Buxtehuder Bulle, the Bay Area Book Reviewers' Association Award for Children's Literature, the Arizona Young Readers' Teen Award, and the South Carolina Junior Readers' Award, as well as being named a Newbery Honor Book, a Michael L. Printz Award Book, an ALA Notable Children's Book, and an ALA Best Book for Young Adults—surprisingly little has been written about it. The novel was reviewed in 2002 when it was published in hardcover, but no formal criticism of the novel appeared in the first decade after the book's publication.

Still, the critics' praise was nearly unanimous. *Kirkus Reviews* calls the novel a "must-read" for science fiction fans, citing Farmer's "talent for creating exciting tales in beautifully realized, unusual worlds." In a starred review, *Publishers Weekly* praises the book for raising questions that "will haunt readers long after the final page." However, the review in *Publishers Weekly* is not alone in quarrelling with the novel's ending, which it labels "rushed." Barbara Scotto, writing for *Horn Book*, praises Farmer's "great imagination in creating a unique and plausible view of the future" but finds that in the conclusion "all problems are resolved in an ending that seems too good to be true." Roger Sutton, writing for the *New York Times Book* Review, agrees that "while the question of Matt's humanity drives the novel, it gets answered and then dropped too easily"; he concludes that the novel is a "big ambitious tale" that raises "questions of literature."

What Do I Read Next?

- On July 24, 2012, Farmer announced in the blog on her home page that she had finished writing and revising the sequel to *The House of the Scorpion*. The book, to be called *The Lord of Opium*, is expected to be published in the fall of 2013.

- Farmer's fifth novel, *A Girl Named Disaster* (1996), is set in Africa, where Farmer lived while she was writing the novel. It tells the story of twelve-year-old Nhamo, from a small village in Mozambique, who must travel alone down the river to her father's people in Zimbabwe. During her year-long journey, she struggles with hunger, animal attacks, and loneliness, relying mainly on her own intelligence and the guidance of spirits.

- In Margaret Peterson Haddix's *Double Identity* (2005), twelve-year-old Bethany is sent away from her parents to live with her aunt. There she learns that her parents had an older daughter, Elizabeth, who died in a car accident, and that Bethany is a clone created to replace her sister.

- *Holes* (1998), by Louis Sachar, won the National Book Award and the 1999 Newbery Medal. It tells the story of Stanley Yelnats, a thirteen-year-old boy, who ends up in a juvenile detention facility. Stanley must learn to deal with extreme physical demands, uncaring supervisors, and tough boys who are afraid to show emotion and become friends.

- M. T. Anderson's satirical novel *Feed* (2002) takes place in a world where almost everyone is directly connected to the Internet through chips implanted in their brains. The story revolves around Titus, a typical teenage boy, and Violet, a girl who has decided to resist the "feed."

- Sherman Alexie's *The Absolutely True Diary of a Part-Time Indian* (2007) tells the story of Arnold "Junior" Spirit, who does not fit in with his Native American peers because of his success at school and his dreams for the future and does not fit in at high school because he is disabled and not white. The controversial novel, which won the National Book Award, follows Junior through difficult times at home and at school, using humor to explore serious issues, including alcoholism and death.

- *After Dolly: The Uses and Misuses of Human Cloning* (2006), by Ian Wilmut and Roger Highfield, tells how scientists created Dolly the sheep, the first cloned mammal, in 1996. It also explores questions about how cloning might be used in medicine and draws a clear line between what the authors find to be ethical and unethical uses.

- *Cloning* (2006), edited by Louise I.

Gerdes, is part of Greenhaven Press's Introducing Issues through Opposing Viewpoints series. It includes fourteen essays that debate the ethics of human cloning, stem cell research, and the cloning of pets and endangered species.

Sources

Cook, Colleen W., *Mexico's Drug Cartels*, Congressional Research Service Report for Congress, October 16, 2007, pp. i, 4.

Farmer, Nancy, Author's Note in *The House of the Scorpion*, Atheneum, 2002, pp. 383–88.

———, "Bio," Nancy Farmer's Official Home Page, http://www.nancyfarmerwebsite.com/bio.html (accessed August 10, 2012).

———, *The House of the Scorpion*, Atheneum, 2002.

———, "Karoshi," Nancy Farmer's Official Home Page, July 24, 2012, http://www.nancyfarmerwebsite.com/ blog.html (accessed July 25, 2012).

Krikorian, Mark, "The Perpetual Border Battle," in *National Interest*, July/August 2012, pp. 44–52.

Marcus, Leonard S., ed. "Nancy Farmer," in *The Wand in the Word: Conversations with Writers of Fantasy*, Candlewick, 2006, pp. 48–61.

Review of *The House of the Scorpion*, in *Kirkus Reviews*, Vol. 70, No. 3, July 1, 2002, p. 954.

Review of *The House of the Scorpion*, in *Publishers Weekly*, Vol. 249, No. 26, July 1, 2002, pp. 80–81.

Scotto, Barbara, Review of *The House of the Scorpion*, in *Horn Book Magazine*, Vol. 78, No. 6,

November/December 2002, pp. 753–54.

Sutton, Roger, "Disorder at the Border," in *New York Times Book Review*, November 17, 2002, p. 39.

Zhuge, Scott, "Going Home: Illegal Immigration Reverses Course," in *Harvard International Review*, Summer 2012, pp. 7–8.

Further Reading

Bould, Mark, *The Routledge Companion to Science Fiction*, Routledge, 2009.

> This reference book gives a solid overview of science fiction. Articles describe major authors and texts, trace subgenres and literary movements, and explain how scholars and readers have approached these works.

Datlow, Ellen, and Terri Windling, eds., *A Wolf at the Door and Other Retold Fairy Tales*, Aladdin, 2000.

> In this collection, thirteen award-winning fantasy and science fiction writers retell familiar fairy tales from new angles. Farmer's contribution is "Falada," a version of "The Goose Girl" narrated by Falada, the horse.

Grant, Richard, *God's Middle Finger: Into the Lawless Heart of the Sierra Madre*, Free Press, 2008.

> In this gritty and dark book, journalist Richard Grant describes the fifteen years he spent in the Sierra Madre mountains, near the border between Mexico and Arizona, and the healers, students, cowboys,

and drug traffickers he encountered there.

Marcus, Leonard S., ed., *The Wand in the Word: Conversations with Writers of Fantasy*, Candlewick Press, 2006.

As the subtitle suggests, this volume contains interviews with thirteen writers of fantasy fiction for young adults, including Farmer, Lloyd Alexander, Susan Cooper, Brian Jacques, and Philip Pullman. In Farmer's chapter, she discusses her childhood reading habits, her laboratory work, and her writing practice.

November, Sharyn, ed., *Firebirds: An Anthology of Original Fantasy and Science Fiction*, Penguin, 2003.

This volume is a collection of sixteen original stories by fantasy and science fiction writers of the twenty-first century, including Lloyd Alexander, Diana Wynne Jones, and Garth Nix. It includes Farmer's story "Remember Me."

Urrea, Luis Alberto, *The Devil's Highway: A True Story*, Little, Brown, 2004.

In 2001, twenty-six men tried to cross the border from Mexico into Arizona, moving through the landscape depicted in *The House of the Scorpion*. As this dramatic book tells, only twelve made it back alive through the rugged terrain.

Suggested Search Terms

Nancy Farmer

House of the Scorpion

science fiction AND cloning

U.S.-Mexico border AND drugs

young-adult AND science fiction

scorpion AND science fiction

Nancy Farmer AND cloning

Nancy Farmer AND science fiction

Nancy Farmer AND scorpion

CPSIA information can be obtained
at www.ICGtesting.com
Printed in the USA
BVHW01s1103090318
510156BV00001B/63/P